How to Train Your Standard Schnauzer

Expert Guide to Smart Socialization Strategies, Caring, Grooming, and Raising an Obedient, Companion Dog

Finnley Crestwood

Disclaimer

The information in this book is intended for general guidance on training French Bulldogs. It is not a substitute for professional advice. Always consult with a veterinarian or certified dog trainer for tailored recommendations. The author and publisher disclaim any liability for actions taken based on the content of this book.

How to Train your
Standard
Schnauzer

Contents

Introduction

With their proud beards and lovable faces, Standard Schnauzers have been bringing joy into people's lives for centuries. These robustly built, intelligent dogs have a larger-than-life personality perfectly suited for farm life - alert, protective, energetic, and trainable. So it's no wonder the Standard Schnauzer was one of the most popular all-around working dog breeds on farms in their native Germany during the Middle Ages!

While their popularity may have waned over the centuries with the onset of industrialization, the adaptable Schnauzer has found new niches in roles like police work, obedience competitions, therapy duties, and most importantly, as a loyal family companion.

My first introduction to the Standard Schnauzer breed was as a young child visiting my Uncle Hans' dairy farm. His two Schnauzers, Otto and Heidi, would enthusiastically herd the cows, stand guard over the chickens, and playfully entertain me for hours. I was amazed at how the clever, good-natured dogs could switch from their serious working mode to being gentle, silly playmates in the blink of an eye. I was smitten!

Decades later when my wife and I were looking for the perfect pet to join our family with young children, my memories of those fond times with my uncle's Schnauzers quickly put the breed at the top of our list. We found a responsible breeder and welcomed home our lively puppy Fritz when the kids were 6 and 8 years old.

Those first few months were filled with both chaos and joy as we worked to housetrain the romping ball of energy that was Fritz. I soon realized that starting training early and establishing clear rules and boundaries were key to harnessing the potential of this highly intelligent breed. Luckily,

Fritz was food-motivated and eager to please, quick to pick up on commands from our positive reinforcement training sessions full of treats and praise.

While still puppies at heart their whole lives, Standard Schnauzers grow into serious-minded, devoted companions. Now 7 years into our journey with Fritz, I can't imagine life without him. He keeps our household feeling safe and provides endless laughs with his playful antics. The kids have grown up with Fritz by their sides through all the ups and downs of childhood. He's been the most perfect family dog we could have hoped for!

In this comprehensive book, I'll share the wealth of hands-on knowledge I've gained about successfully training Standard Schnauzers like Fritz. You'll learn how to: Choose a quality Schnauzer puppy and be prepared for their arrival, Housebreak your pup and teach good manners, Master basic obedience cues through positive training, Curb problematic

Schnauzer behaviors like barking, jumping, or digging, Keep your Schnauzer engaged through games, sports, and puzzles, Provide proper healthcare, nutrition, grooming and exercise, Travel with your Schnauzer and enjoy their golden years.

I'll also share plenty of amusing anecdotes along the way about the silly antics and big personalities of the Schnauzers I've lived with and loved over the years. Consider this book your go-to training manual for welcoming a Standard Schnauzer into your life and forging an unbreakable bond built on mutual understanding, respect, and tons of fun. Let's get started!

Chapter One

Understanding the Standard Schnauzer

Brief History of the Breed

Germany was the birthplace of the Standard Schnauzer, an all-purpose farm dog and ratter that dates back to the 1500s. Probably bred into the dogs on purpose, their distinctive beards and mustaches serve to conceal their faces and eyes from barn rats.

The Schnauzer's name comes from the German term for "snout" because of its characteristically beardless cheeks. Standard, Miniature, and Giant are the three sizes of the Schnauzer breed. The original medium-sized dog was the Standard

Schnauzer, and the miniature variety emerged in the late 19th and early 20th centuries from offspring of smaller Standards. The largest of the three varieties, the Giant Schnauzer is a hybrid of Standard Schnauzers, Great Danes, and German Shepherds.

In the 1800s and beyond, Schnauzers were well-known as dependable farm and home dogs in Germany. They were highly prized for their intelligence, power, ratting abilities, and protective demeanor. The Standard Schnauzer was formally recognized as a breed in 1879.

The Standard Schnauzer was introduced to the United States in the early 1900s. They were classed as part of the Terrier group by the American Kennel Club in 1904 due to their feistiness and ratting history. While less prevalent than many breeds, Schnauzers have been continually popular over the decades, placing currently in the top 50 most popular breeds in the U.S.

Over their lengthy history, Schnauzers have been bred for adaptability. In addition to their traditional tasks on farms, they have served people as police dogs, service dogs, therapy dogs, search & rescue dogs, and devoted family companions. Their intelligence and drive to please have allowed them to flourish across different job roles.

Temperament and Personality

The Standard Schnauzer has a temperament that combines high intelligence, enthusiasm, devotion, protectiveness, and fun-loving playfulness. Properly socialized and trained, they make ideal family dogs with moderate exercise needs.

Intelligence and trainability are defining traits of the Schnauzer. They are rapid learners and very responsive to positive reinforcement training and rewards. Schnauzers flourish when provided with plenty of mental stimulation and tasks. Without adequate activity, kids may become bored and disruptive.

Schnauzers build deep ties with their families. They seek to please and appreciate the responsibility of numerous chores around the home. Obedience training is suggested to establish rules and boundaries with your Schnauzer from a young age.

The Schnauzer personality is lively and eager. They adore games, toys, and connecting with their family. Affectionate and playful, they appreciate being near their owners. Schnauzers sometimes have a wicked sense of humor and keep their families delighted.

While dedicated to their people, Standard Schnauzers can be initially suspicious of strangers. They have modest protective instincts and may bark to inform their family of anything unexpected. With socialization and training, they can learn to accept guests correctly.

Some Schnauzers can be obstinate, stubborn, or bossy. Establishing your function as a calm, consistent pack leader is vital. Schnauzers may test limits and need reminders of regulations. Obedience training helps reinforce commands.

Overall, the Standard Schnauzer personality is fun-loving, intelligent, energetic, and driven. They genuinely enjoy being part of an active family, partaking in play, training, exercise, and bonding events. With their working dog heritage, they thrive when given chores and challenges to keep their busy minds engaged.

Physical Characteristics

The Standard Schnauzer has a particular physical appearance typified by their tough double coat, distinctive beard and eyebrows, docked tail, and square proportions. Their weather-resistant coat and athletic physique allowed them to perform farm work in all types of terrain and climates.

Standard Schnauzers stand 17 to 19 inches tall at the shoulder and weigh 30 to 50 pounds as adults. Males are generally larger and taller than females. The physique is squarely proportioned, compact, and sturdy. Sturdy legs and robust feet lend themselves to a lively, trotting pace.

Their head is powerful and rectangular with a pronounced stop, flat skull, and strong muzzle. The medium-sized, almond-shaped eyes are dark brown. V-shaped ears stand erect when clipped or fold over naturally. Expression is characterized by bushy eyebrows and a beard and mustache.

The wiry, dense coat is salt and pepper or fully black in color. It has a soft, thick undercoat with a rough, wiry outer coat around 1 to 2 inches long. The coat is often hand-stripped for maximum texture. The face, ears, and legs have shorter fur. The tail is docked to half length.

The weather-resistant double coat provides protection and allows the Schnauzer to thrive as an energetic working dog in all climes. Regular brushing and hand-stripping limit matting and shedding. Overall, the Standard Schnauzer's distinctive design reflects its traditional duties - the beard protected the face, the dense coat permitted adaptability, the docked tail prevented injuries, and the square body provided strength and stamina for work.

Chapter Three

Bringing Your Schnauzer Puppy Home

Supplies You'll Need

Preparing for a new Schnauzer puppy demands obtaining specific materials ahead of time to assist the puppy settle into your home comfortably and starting the training process straight away. Here are some of the crucial materials you'll want to have ready before taking your Schnauzer puppy home:

- **Crate** - A crate provides a great sleeping and resting location for a puppy and is very useful for house training. Get a crate sized for an adult Schnauzer to give room to grow. Include a nice cage pad and chew toys.

- **Dog bed** - Provide a comfy dog bed for sleeping in the main living areas and bedrooms. This gives the pet a comfy space to slumber and lounge near the family.

- **Bowls** - Get a set of stainless steel or ceramic food and water bowls. Shallow dishes are great for pups.

- **Collar & leash** - A correctly fitted flat collar and 6-foot leash are important for walks, tags, and control. A martingale collar is also helpful for training.

- **ID tag** - Put an ID tag with your contact data on the pup's collar as soon as possible for safety.

- **Puppy food** - Buy a high-quality puppy feed to adequately nourish your Schnauzer puppy. Feed the amount indicated on the box.

- **snacks** - Have an assortment of healthy training snacks like little chunks of chicken, cheese, or commercial goodies. Avoid too many sugary foods.

- **Chew toys** - Provide a selection of quality chew toys to suit the pup's demands for stimulation and healing sore gums.

- **Brush** - Invest in a quality slicker brush, undercoat rake, and comb for combing the wiry Schnauzer coat.

- **Nail clipper** - Clip puppy nails monthly to encourage good habits. Use styptic powder in case of nicking the quick.

- **Cleaning supplies** - Enzyme cleaner, paper towels, and stain/odor remover are needed for unavoidable accidents during housetraining.

- **Baby gates** - Use gates to block off areas and keep the puppy within sight. This aids with supervision during house training.

- **Puppy playpen** - A playpen provides a safe, contained space for the puppy while you're away. Include potty pads, toys, and water.

Picking out and gathering materials ahead of time makes the transition smoother when you first bring the puppy home. It allows you to focus on bonding, training, and helping the newest member of your family settle in securely.

Puppy-Proofing Your Home

Before your Schnauzer puppy arrives, take time to completely puppy-proof your home. This prevents destructive chewing difficulties or the puppy from eating something dangerous. Key areas to focus on include:

- **Remove loose goods, clutter, and trash** - Put away loose papers, knickknacks, shoes, clothing, trash cans, etc. that may tempt chewing or become destroyed.

- **Lift low-hanging wires** - Raise any electrical cords out of the puppy's reach to reduce chewing concerns. Tuck wires behind furniture.

- **Secure houseplants** - Move houseplants to high shelves so the curious pup won't dig or devour. Many common plants are poisonous to dogs.

- **Block off prohibited areas** - Use baby gates to keep the puppy away from places like the kitchen or laundry room where dangerous cleaners or machinery may reside.

- **Stow bathroom supplies** - Secure any bathroom towels, plungers, or toilet paper that can turn into a play object for shredding.

- **Remove drugs** - Ensure human medications, vitamins, etc. are stored away where the puppy cannot access them.

- **Take out garbage** - Empty all trash cans frequently so there's nothing tempting for the puppy to scavenge.

- **Limit access to valuables** - Stow away objects like shoes, clothing, pillows, remote controls, books, etc. to prevent damage.

- **Check for gaps** - Seal off any potential openings behind appliances or beneath fences where a pup may escape or become stuck.

- **Ensure latched doors/cabinets** - Latch closed cupboards and doors to areas the puppy shouldn't access like the pantry or laundry.

- **Cover sharp table edges** - Protect the puppy from injury by cushioning sharp table/furniture edges with corner coverings.

Taking the time to puppy-proof fully lowers temptation and helps set your Schnauzer pup up for success during training. Revisit occasionally as the dog matures. Preventing incorrect chewing today helps avoid damaging habits long-term.

Finding a Reputable Breeder or Rescue

Finding a competent Standard Schnauzer breeder or rescue is vital to ensure a happy, healthy dog. Be selective in your choice. Here's what to look for:

- **Health testing** - Reputable breeders do recommend OFA health screening on parent dogs for concerns like hip dysplasia. Ask for proof.

- **Temperament** - Good breeders focus on creating dogs with stable, amiable temperaments. Meet parent dogs.

- **Clean facilities** - The breeder's facility should be clean, roomy, and puppy-proofed. This indicates proper care.

- **AKC registration** - While not the primary qualification, AKC registration displays adherence to breed standards.

- **Written contract** - The breeder should give a clear written contract describing expectations, replacements, etc.

- **Interview breeder** - Talk to the breeder thoroughly. Ask lots of questions about parent dogs, socializing, experience, etc.

- **Puppy raising procedures** - puppies should be nurtured inside, handled regularly, and exposed to varied stimuli for optimum development.

- **Vet care/shots** - The breeder should provide a record of each puppy's vet appointments and immunizations. The first batch of shots should already be administered.

- **Puppy packet** - Reputable breeders send new owner packs with vet records, food samples, pedigree details, and training/care guidance.

For rescues, search for:

- **Vetting of dogs** - The rescue should fully vet each dog for health and temperament prior to adoption.

- **Adoption procedure** - Reputable rescues have an application and screening process to ensure appropriate matches.

- **Contract or agreement** - Review the rescue's adoption contract completely to understand requirements.

- **help resources** - Good rescues provide new adoptive help and training/care resources to set you up for success.

Finding an ethical, responsible provider for your Schnauzer can help your puppy get off to a good start for a long, healthy, happy life as your friend. Take your time studying choices. Don't support puppy mills or pet retailers.

Chapter Three

Bringing Your Schnauzer Puppy Home

Pick-up Day Tips

Picking up your Schnauzer puppy and taking them home for the first time is exciting. Here are some recommendations to ensure the puppy pick-up day goes smoothly:

- **Puppy-proof vehicle** - Line the backseat with pee pads and bring a crate/carrier secured with a seatbelt for safety. Bring potty pads for stops.

- **Collar/leash** - Use a collar and leash to walk your puppy instead of carrying, so they learn to walk properly on leash from the start.

- **ID tag** - Make sure your puppy is wearing a collar with an ID tag for the trip home and at all times afterward.

- **Transport safely** - Never allow your pup to go loose in the vehicle. Use a carrier or cage secured with a seatbelt.

- **Stop for toilet breaks** - Plan to stop every hour or two to let your dog potty and stretch their legs. Offer water.

- **Provide toys** - Bring safe chew toys to engage your pet during the trip home. This lowers anxiety and chewing impulses.

- **Be calm and soothing** - Speak gently and reassuringly if your dog seems scared. Some sobbing is normal. Offer sweets and toys for diversion.

- **Limit interaction** - Advise family and friends to wait to meet the puppy once home and settle to avoid overwhelming them initially.

- **Set up a safe area** - Have an enclosure, box, or confined safe space set up at home with food, drink, pads, and toys for instant use upon arrival.

- **Introduce carefully** - Once home, gently introduce your new Schnauzer to their new home a room at a time, keeping things low key.

- **Supervise closely** - Do not leave your new puppy unsupervised, even for a few minutes, as accidents or gnawing can happen quickly.

- **Be positive** - Praise and reward favorable behaviors right away to reinforce training. Your puppy is learning rapidly at this age.

Picking up your new Schnauzer puppy is the start of an incredible journey together. With careful planning and care on puppy pick-up day, you'll be setting your relationship up for success.

First Night Settlement

The first night home with your new Schnauzer puppy is joyful yet takes patience. Here are some ways to help your dog settle in easily on their first night:

- **Feed a familiar meal** - Stick with the same food the breeder or rescue was feeding initially to keep the diet constant during the changeover.

- **Take outside frequently** - Expect to take your puppy outside to potty every 1-2 hours initially, including overnight. Praise for going in the right area.

- **Supervise constantly** - Do not leave the pup unaccompanied inside for any length to prevent accidents. Watch for sniffing, circling, or squatting.

- **Use the crate for sleeping** - Have the pup sleep in a crate at night next to your bed. This eliminates overnight accidents and makes them feel secure.

- **Provide a comfy bed** - Place a cuddly, comfortable dog bed with familiar scents from the breeder/rescue in the crate at night.

- **Be reassuring if weeping** - Some fussing the first night is typical. Reassure the puppy gently if crying and take it outdoors to potty. Avoid too much attention.

- **Limit first-day interaction** - Introduce your Schnauzer to your home and family members gradually on the first day. Overstimulation is prevalent.

- **Set up safe space** - When you can't actively observe, place the pup in a gated area or playpen with toys, pads, and water to prevent trouble.

- **Keep calm energy** - Be calm and consistent in your energy and approach with the puppy. Anxiety is frequent the first night; be reassuring.

- **Start training** - Use the first days and nights at home to start reinforcing fundamental training including name, potty training, basic commands, and manners.

- **Be patient** - Accidents and screaming during the night are common initially. With routine, monitoring, and training, your pup will adjust to its new home.

The first night with a new puppy takes adjusting. Set your Schnauzer and yourself up for success by planning sleeping arrangements and developing a routine for meals, training, and spending time together.

Introducing to Other Pets

Integrating a new Schnauzer puppy into a home with existing pets requires planning and patience for a safe, effective transition. Here are some tips:

- **Separate at first** - Keep current pets and new puppies isolated initially. Let them get acclimated to odors and sounds while supervised. Exchange blankets.

- **Arrange introductions** - Start introductions outside on neutral territory during short, scheduled sessions. Keep dogs leashed under supervision.

- **Watch intently** - Monitor all encounters carefully for any symptoms of fear, hostility, or dominant behaviors. Interrupt if needed.

- **Pet current pets first** - Make a point to pet and praise resident pets first before the new puppy to avoid jealousy. Give snacks.

- **Provide individual attention** - Ensure your existing pets still get quality one-on-one play, walks, and snuggle time following the new addition.

- **Establish hierarchy** - Reinforce the hierarchy with existing pets first. The new dog must understand their place is at the bottom to prevent fights.

- **Share toys/goodies** - Once accepting, train dogs to share toys and take treats respectfully under your supervision so positive habits are developed.

- **Allow space** - Make sure each pet has an area they can go to and have alone time when needed.

- **Be patient** - It can take weeks or longer for a seamless adjustment, especially with an elderly resident pet. Go gradually.

- **Consult trainer** - If major aggression issues occur, seek aid from a professional trainer or behaviorist for guidance.

Proper planning, patience, and consistency are crucial when merging a new puppy into a multi-pet family. Provide reassurance and assistance to help all your dogs welcome the new family member smoothly.

Chapter Four

House Training Your Schnauzer

Setting Up a Routine

Establishing a consistent routine is vital for house training your Schnauzer puppy successfully. Puppies thrive on regular schedules for food, potty breaks, training, play, and sleep. Here are guidelines for setting up an efficient routine:

- **Feed on schedule** - Feed your puppy at the same times daily. Feed 3-4 small meals for puppies under 6 months, then graduate to 2 meals a day.

- **Potty first thing** - Take the puppy outside soon upon waking up, after napping, after play, and every 30-60 minutes at first. Praise for going in the right area.

- **Nap regularly** - Enforce nap times in the crate multiple times per day to help prevent accidents. Puppies need 18-20 hours of sleep daily.

- **Consistent toilet site** - Always take the pooch to the same designated outside potty spot and use a command like "Go potty." This trains them where to go.

- **Reward accomplishments** - When puppy potties are outdoors, provide an immediate reward of praise, treatment, and play to reinforce the desirable behavior.

- **Limit freedom** - When unsupervised, keep the puppy confined to a crate or small room with toilet pads if needed. Expand space rights as training develops.

- **Limit water before bed** - Pick up water bowls about 2 hours before bedtime to help minimize nighttime accidents.

- **Evening routine** - Make going pee the last activity before bedtime. Take the pup out on leash; praise for going, then settle into the crate.

- **Adjust for changes** - If your schedule changes, allow more frequent pee breaks until the puppy adapts. Consistency is crucial.

Be cautious and patient. Stick to the regimen rigorously, and accidents in the house will reduce over time as your Schnauzer's bladder control strengthens.

Crate Training

Using a crate properly is highly useful for house training your Schnauzer puppy. The key steps of crate training include:

- **Select crate size** - Get a crate big enough for your Schnauzer to stand, turn around, and lie down in comfortably. Too huge promotes accidents.

- **Make it inviting** - Place a soft crate pad or bed inside, along with a familiar toy. Keep near family activity.

- **Use consistently** - Have the pup sleep in the crate overnight and take supervised naps there during the day.

- **Keep it positive** - Avoid using the crate only for punishment. Make it a safe den. Give food and toys in the crate. Feed meals inside.

- **Close door momentarily** - As your puppy relaxes inside with the door open, practice closing briefly, then rewarding calm behavior.

- **Crate when unsupervised** - When you can't actively oversee your pup, place them in the crate with a toy to prevent accidents.

- **Keep sessions short** - Limit time to a few hours for extremely young pups. Take outside immediately after being freed.

- **Ignore complaints** - If the puppy whines or fusses, resist letting it out till quiet. Reward silence.

- **Provide exercise first** - Take your puppy outside for a pee break and play before crating to tire them out.

- **Make it positive** - Never use the crate for punishment. The idea is for your Schnauzer to cherish the crate as a calm retreat.

With patience and appealing treats, your Schnauzer puppy will learn to rest peacefully in their crate, setting them up for success with house training.

Dealing with Accidents

Accidents are unavoidable while house training a puppy. When they happen, respond effectively to minimize setbacks:

- **Interrupt swiftly** - If you catch your puppy in the process of an accident, interrupt with a firm "No" or distracting sound, then immediately remove them outdoors. Praise for finishing outdoors.

- **Don't penalize after the fact** - Don't criticize or punish your dog for an accident that's already happened, or they may conceal when needing to potty.

- **Clean thoroughly** - Use an enzymatic cleaner where accidents occur to reduce odors that may invite repeat mistakes. Vinegar and hydrogen peroxide also work.

- **Adjust monitoring** - Accidents signal a need for closer supervision and more frequent toilet breaks. Keep your Schnauzer beside you on a leash or crated.

- **Rule out medical problems** - If frequent accidents remain despite close supervision, have your puppy inspected by a vet to rule out a possible urinary tract infection or other condition.

- **Revert training** - For an older puppy with persistent poor habits, go back to housetraining basics by restricting freedom, setting a routine, and rewarding outdoor toilets.

- **Be patient** - Understand accidents will happen as part of the training process. Stick with routines diligently. As bladder control increases, mistakes will reduce.

- **Add encouragement** - After an accident, once cleaned, bring your pup to the same spot and praise suitable potty to establish good habits.

Stay positive through the obstacles of house training. Consistency and time will pay off as your Schnauzer learns desired potty behaviors.

Chapter Five

Basic Obedience Training

The Importance of Socialization

Proper early socialization is vital to creating a nice, confident Schnauzer puppy. It entails carefully introducing puppies to a wide variety of sights, noises, people, animals, and experiences within the peak socialization window - 6 to 14 weeks old. Here are tips:

- **Expose to sounds** - Play audio of vacuum cleaners, cars, sirens, thunderstorms, crowds, and other noises at low levels to desensitize your puppy. Give incentives for calm reactions.

- **Meet new people** - Arrange for your Schnauzer puppy to mingle with individuals of all ages, appearances, and backgrounds. Ask friends over. Go to parks. Give snacks at introductions.

- **Experience surroundings** - Safely expose your pup to different areas like pet stores, autos, elevators, stairs, slippery surfaces, etc. Make it entertaining with praise and toys. Go slowly if scared.

- **Socialize with animals** - Arrange controlled meetings with vaccinated, friendly dogs and cats to teach good manners and suppress reactivity. Supervise closely.

- **Limit unpleasant experiences** - Try to prevent scary or unfavorable social interactions that may traumatize your puppy at this important development stage. Build confidence.

- **Use goodies as an incentive** - Bring delectable snacks on expeditions to associate new sights and sounds with pleasant rewards and influence desired behaviors.

- **Be protective as needed** - If your puppy seems terrified, take them up and retreat to a comfortable distance while their confidence builds. Go slowly.

- **Sign up for puppy lessons** - Enroll in positive reinforcement puppy classes for organized socialization with other puppies and humans under expert instruction.

- **Keep it pleasant** - Ensure socializing outings are joyful, planned, and paired with favorite treats so your Schnauzer builds confidence, not dread.

Thoughtful socialization helps for kinder, better-adapted Schnauzers. Expose your puppy completely during this excellent window to prevent shyness or reactivity concerns later on.

Teaching Basic Cues Like Sit, Stay, Come

It's crucial to start training your Schnauzer puppy fundamental behavior cues like sit, stay, and come from an early age. Here are useful techniques:

- **Use reward-based methods** - Always train using rewards like cookies, praise, and toys. Avoid punishment, which slows learning.

- **Keep sessions brief** - Only train for 5-10 minutes at a time for young puppies. End on successes to create confidence.

- **Get the pup's attention** - Say the puppy's name and show a treat. Repeat cues consistently before rewarding.

- **Reinforce achievements immediately** - When the puppy does the required behavior, mark it with a "yes!" or click, then treat it within 1-2 seconds so they understand.

- **Build in modest increments** - For "sit," hold the treat over the nose and move it back towards the tail when you say "sit." Mark and reward sit. Gradually expect longer sits before treatment.

- **Make stay entertaining** - Ask for small "stays" of a few seconds initially before rewarding. Build up duration gradually, interspersing stays during gaming sessions.

- **Recall off-leash** - For solid "come" when called, reward with high-value treats and big praise. Never penalize for coming.

- **Correct softly** - If the puppy is confused, gently assist them into the right stance when offering cues like sit. Don't force.

- **Use real-life rewards** - When the puppy begins learning cues reliably, phase down continual treat rewards. Reward periodically with food, attention, or access to toys, walks, and play instead.

- **Practice consistency** - Ensure all family members utilize the same cue words and training strategies to avoid confusion.

With regular brief sessions full of positivity, your Schnauzer puppy will rapidly begin understanding the basic cues that make training and life together joyful.

Leash Training

Leash training is a vital skill for Standard Schnauzers to master. Here are guidelines for teaching your puppy to walk politely on a leash:

- **Use suitable equipment** - Choose a lightweight 4-6 foot leash meant for pups and a properly fitted flat collar, slip collar, or harness to avoid harm.

- **Start early** - Begin leash training as soon as your puppy's final round of vaccines is complete, usually around 12-14 weeks old. Don't wait.

- **Make it entertaining** - Introduce the leash and collar through games and treats so they have pleasant connections.

- **Practice in-house first** - Let your puppy trail the leash about indoors and outdoors in a confined area to get used to the feel before genuine leash walking.

- **Use sweets as lures** - Bring delectable food on hikes. Lure your pup into a heel stance, then praise. Use a directive like "let's go" to reinforce.

- **Go at the puppy's pace** - Walk depending on your puppy's energy level. Follow their lead at first as they sniff and explore, letting them adjust.

- **Incorporate training** - Work on cues like sit, remain, and come during walks. Change pace and direction often to develop responsiveness.

- **Be patient** - Puppies will wander, become distracted, and resist at times. Stay calm. Keep hikes brief and rewarding.

- **Remove for tantrums** - If your puppy starts tantruming, stop moving and become uninterested until they quit, then restart the walk.

With consistency, patience, and rewards, leash training will rapidly become second nature to your Standard Schnauzer, setting you both up for delightful walks together.

Chapter Six

Stopping Unwanted Behaviors

Barking, Digging, Jumping Up

Schnauzers are prone to various unwanted behaviors like barking, digging, and jumping up. Here are some practical strategies to curb these habits:

For barking: - Identify triggers - Monitor to determine what provokes excess barking like sights, sounds, guests, being left alone, etc.

• **Address underlying issues** - If barking arises from fear, anxiety, boredom, or excess energy, address the main cause with training, exercise, and enrichment.

- **Teach "quiet" command** - Use a reward marker like a clicker when your Schnauzer stops barking, then reward with food. This teaches them to stop on demand.

- **Distract with toys** - Redirect your Schnauzer's impulse to bark into a chew toy to occupy their mouth. Stuff a Kong with their food during trigger times.

- **Block access to stimuli** - Close drapes and blinds to obscure external triggers. Muffle sounds that provoke barking. Keep your Schnauzer away from fences/doors where they bark at passersby.

- **Use a corrective device** - Spray anti-bark collars or sonic/ultrasonic bark deterrents to detect and terminate excessive barking automatically. Use cautiously.

- **Avoid screams or punishment** - Yelling at a barking Schnauzer might actually reinforce the habit. Stay cool, redirect to a toy, or command "quiet" instead.

For digging:

- **Provide authorized digging site** - Designate a dog-friendly area of loose earth or sand where your Schnauzer can dig without issue. Bury toys for them to uncover.

- **Fence off limits** - Restrict your Schnauzer's access to any garden beds or off-limits digging zones via fencing or monitoring.

- **Exercise more** - Ensure your Schnauzer gets appropriate exercise and enrichment. Digging can happen while bored.

- **Watch for signs** - When you see digging body language such as sniffing, circling, or pawing, interrupt and redirect to a chew toy instead.

- **impede the attempt** - Place large rocks or chicken wire over areas you don't want to be dug up to impede the ability.

- **Keep indoors while unaccompanied** - Don't leave your Schnauzer outside alone if they repeatedly dig. Supervise or crate indoors instead.

For jumping up:

- **Ignore undesirable behavior** - Turn away and divert focus when the pup jumps. When they sit calmly, reward them with affection.

- **Teach incompatible behavior** - Train "sit" or "off" commands using goodies. Require your Schnauzer to sit before receiving pets or attention.

- **Avoid yelling or kneeing** - Never punish leaping by yelling or kneeing your Schnauzer, as this might provoke bites and increase excitement. Withdraw attention smoothly instead.

- **Praise good manners** - Whenever your pup approaches respectfully without jumping, provide goodies, praise, and affection to reinforce the habit.

- **Pet from above** - Stand upright and reach down to pet your Schnauzer rather than leaning over, which can provoke jumping.

With positive training methods focused on reinforcing incompatible good behaviors, your Schnauzer can overcome these bad tendencies. Be patient and consistent.

Separation Anxiety

Schnauzers are prone to experiencing separation anxiety that leads to destructive behavior when left alone. Here are some preventative and management tips:

- **Establish independence early** - Get your Schnauzer used to alone time and separation from you during puppyhood through crate training and solo play times.

- **Tire before departures** - Take your dog on a brisk walk or play session before leaving to take the edge off and lessen pent-up energy.

- **Use soothing pheromones** - Try calming pheromone sprays, diffusers, or collars during periods alone to relieve anxiousness. Products like Adaptil are proven to help.

- **Provide interactive toys** - When leaving your dog, provide intriguing puzzle toys loaded with treats to serve as distractions.

- **Maintain routines** - Stick to normal timetables for meals, walks, and departures/arrivals as much as possible so the time alone becomes predictable.

- **Avoid emotional hellos/goodbyes** - Come and go in a calm, low-key manner rather than unduly accentuating your entrance or departure.

- **Crate train** - Dogs frequently feel more secure and comfortable in a crate when left alone. Introduce gradually with prizes and rewards.

- **Try anti-anxiety medicine** - In severe cases, ask your vet about anti-anxiety medication that may help ease your dog's distress when left alone.

- **Consult a trainer** - A trainer can advise you in desensitizing your Schnauzer to your absences through gradual exposure training.

- **Rule out medical problems** - Have your vet examine your Schnauzer to verify no underlying physical concerns are causing the behavior.

With time, patience, and constructive ways, your Schnauzer can learn to feel content spending non-excessive time alone without anxiety or destruction. Seek expert help if the condition persists.

Aggression Towards Other Dogs

Dog aggressiveness is a breed characteristic among some Schnauzers that requires special training and supervision. Here are ways to limit this behavior:

- **Socialize extensively early** - Ensure your Schnauzer puppy meets friendly, vaccinated dogs routinely throughout the vital socialization stage of 6-14 weeks old.

- **Avoid dog parks** - Dog parks are high-risk owing to overstimulation and inability to moderate interactions. Stick to play dates with gentler dogs.

- **Stay watchful on walks** - When walking on a leash, create distance from approaching dogs and use incentives to maintain your Schnauzer's focus on you.

- **Obedience training** - Solid obedience skills like "look at me," "sit" and "stay" increase your control and snap your dog's attention away from triggers. Practice around distractions.

- **Address underlying fear** - If your Schnauzer's aggression looks frightening in nature, gradual counterconditioning can help shift the emotional response. Consult a trainer.

- **Walk away from problems** - If an approaching off-leash dog gets your Schnauzer heated up, simply walk away quietly to defuse rather than allow a fight.

- **Muzzle when needed** - Basket-style muzzles worn during walks or contact with dogs lessen bite danger. Introduce progressively with positive conditioning.

- **Consider medication** - In severe circumstances, medication given by a vet may help take the edge off your Schnauzer's violent attitude. Use alongside training.

- **Hire trainer/behaviorist** - Professional assistance targeted to your Schnauzer's individual triggers and behaviors can be invaluable for learning management and modification tactics.

With management considerations and specialized desensitization training, Schnauzers can dramatically improve dog aggression and at minimum learn to tolerate polite dog encounters. Be consistent and patient.

Chapter Seven

Schnauzer Grooming Essentials

Brushing, Clipping, Bathing

The wiry double coat of the Schnauzer requires frequent grooming to look clean and prevent matting. Key grooming tasks include:

Brushing: - Invest in tools - A slicker brush and metal comb are needed for penetrating the Schnauzer coat. A rake can help remove loose hairs.

- **Brush often** - Ideally brush your Schnauzer 2-3 times each week from skin out to promote the coat and remove debris.

- **Watch body language** - Go slowly if your dog seems to be touch sensitive. Give rewards and praise to make grooming fun.

- **Work in portions** - Break the body into sections when brushing to be thorough - legs, tummy, back, sides, etc.

- **Follow coat direction** - Always brush in the direction the fur grows naturally to avoid tugging the coat. Work any matting out gradually.

- **Check feet** - Extend the legs forward to clean and look between toes where material collects.

Clipping: - Research styles - There are numerous typical Schnauzer clips including the pet clip, display clip, or puppy clip. Choose one that suits your needs.

- **Invest in tools** - Quality clippers made for wiry coats are a requirement. #10 blades perform well for the close Schnauzer cut. Have clipper oil handy.

- **Remove mats first** - Carefully brush out any mats before attempting to clip the coat. Mats restrict the clippers from gliding easily.

- **Work methodically** - Start at the rear and clip one side at a time. Lift the leg and clip the belly, chest, and front last.

- **Blend edges** - Blend and taper the borders of cut regions so the transition seems smooth.

- **Clean feet** - Clip the hair between pads and trim nails. Hair left between toes can lead to debris getting trapped.

Bathing: - Use suitable shampoo - Opt for a high-quality shampoo suited for wiry, dense coats. Avoid human shampoos that dry the skin.

- **Bathe as needed** - Only bathe your Schnauzer every 4-6 weeks or when soiled. Overbathing removes the coat's oils.

- **Dry thoroughly** - Use a high-velocity dryer on a lower heat setting to dry the dense undercoat completely. Air dry the rest. Check for moisture.

- **Brush after bath** - Always brush the coat completely after bathing to prevent matting as it dries.

Regularly adhering to your Schnauzer's particular grooming needs minimizes skin concerns, lowers shedding, and keeps them looking handsome.

Nail Trimming, Ear Cleaning

In addition to coat care, nail, and ear care are key elements of the Schnauzer grooming routine.

Nail Trimming Tips:

- **Use suitable trimmers** - Invest in quality guillotine dog nail clippers suited for black nails. Change blades yearly.

- **Have styptic handy** - Always keep styptic powder or gel on hand. Applying it will stop bleeding if you nick the quick.

- **Sit or lay the dog down** - Have someone gently hold your Schnauzer sitting or lying belly up to keep them motionless and expose nails.

- **Hold foot steady** - Gently grab a front paw to extend the leg forward for greater access. Secure each toe to clip.

- **Clip below quick** - Trim just the transparent area of the nail below the pink quick within. Only take off a small quantity at a time.

- **Grind down** - Use a nail grinder after clipping to soften sharp edges and steadily diminish the quick's length with vibration.

- **Reward collaboration** - Give gifts before and after to make nail care a good experience rather than a conflict.

Ear Cleaning Tips:

- **Use adequate cleaner** - Never use cotton swabs inside. Vet-approved cleaners disintegrate wax for safe removal.

- **Inspect first** - Before cleaning, softly peep inside ears to check for redness, discharge, or bad odor indicating potential infection. Seek veterinary assessment if present.

- **Apply cleanser** - Squirt vet-approved ear wash or cleansing wipe into the ear canal and gently massage the base of the ear.

- **Let the dog shake** - Allow your Schnauzer to shake their head to work the cleanser further into the canal.

- **Wipe out** - Use cotton balls to gently wipe away extra debris and fluid from the inner ear flap. Repeat with dry cotton to eliminate wetness.

- **Check after** - Ensure you've removed all visible wax and debris from the ear canal after cleaning.

- **Reward your dog** - Give goodies and praise for cooperative conduct during ear cleaning.

Regular nail and ear upkeep keeps your Schnauzer happy and free of preventable infections caused by trapped moisture, dirt, and growing nails.

Finding a Professional Groomer

Having a qualified professional groomer maintain your Schnauzer's coat is beneficial. Here are recommendations for picking a top-notch groomer:

- **Ask breeders** - Reputable Schnauzer breeders generally have good groomers they recommend and utilize for their dogs.

- **Seek referrals** - Talk to Schnauzer owners in your neighborhood about groomers they love. Visit pets in person to evaluate the grooming quality.

- **Confirm experience** - Choose an expert groomer who is well familiar with the Schnauzer coat, clips, and skin needs.

- **Evaluate facility** - Visit the shop in advance. It should appear clean, organized, and professional. How are the dogs handled?

- **Discuss services** - Talk to the groomer about exactly the services you want for your Schnauzer and the approximate time frame. Voice any concerns.

- **Assess handling skills** - Observe how your Schnauzer behaves to the groomer upon first contact. Do they appear competent handling the dog?

- **Stick with the same groomer** - Using the same groomer constantly encourages your dog to get comfortable. It enables the groomer to discover your dog's quirks.

- **Provide directions** - Inform the groomer of any sensitivities, skin issues, injuries, or behaviors to watch for. Update as needed.

- **Tip wisely** - Tip your groomer 15-20% of the entire amount provided they did outstanding service and handled your dog nicely.

Finding a talented groomer you and your Schnauzer trust make grooming a breeze while ensuring your dog looks and feels their best.

Chapter Eight

Exercise and Mental Stimulation

Importance of Daily Activity

As an energetic working breed, Standard Schnauzers require extensive daily exercise and mental enrichment. Ensuring proper activity helps avoid undesirable habits.

- **Health benefits** - Regular exercise keeps Schnauzers physically active and at a healthy weight while preventing obesity and associated disorders.

- **Mental stimulation** - Schnauzers flourish when their clever minds are challenged through training, engaging play, and solving puzzles. Boredom leads to devastation.

- **Behavior improvements** - Schnauzers who get appropriate activity every day tend to be calmer, more trainable, and less prone to hyperactivity disorders. Exercise reduces pent-up energy.

- **Bonding** - Participating together in walks, playtime, and training enhances the link between Schnauzer and the owner. They crave time with their family.

- **Socialization** - Getting out for daily leashed walks and play time enables continued beneficial exposure to new sights, noises, canines, and people. This inhibits over-protectiveness and reactive tendencies.

- **Energy outlet** - Schnauzers have naturally high energy. Without useful outlets like exercise, they are prone to undesirables like excessive barking, digging, and gnawing.

- **Obedience practice** - The walks, play, and training sessions of each day provide vital real-world practice for reinforcing instructions, manners, and attentiveness.

- **Joint health** - Moderate, low-impact exercise can help maintain joint health and mobility, delaying disorders like arthritis that might develop in some Schnauzers.

Aim for at least 60-90 minutes of activity every day for a Standard Schnauzer in the form of stimulating walks, playing, training sessions, or another exercise. Keep their minds and bodies challenged!

Fun Games and Toys for Indoor Play

In addition to outdoor exercise, it's crucial to engage your Standard Schnauzer in interactive indoor play every day to challenge their brains and work off energy. Great games and toys include:

- **Tug** - This satisfies a Schnauzer's instinctive passion of "killing" prey like rodents. Use a rope toy and participate in short pulling bursts, practicing 'drop it' command.

- **Fetch** - Tossing balls or flying disc toys for them to retrieve and engage their strong prey drive. Practice commands like remain, wait, come, and drop it.

- **Hide and seek** - Have your Schnauzer sit-stay while you hide a toy, then say "Find it!" so they may use their nose to seek it out. Increase difficulty by hiding rewards throughout a room instead.

- **Busy box puzzles** - Puzzle toys that need manipulation with paws and nose to uncover hidden food promote cerebral stimulation and physical activity. Introduce gently.

- **Snuffle mats** - These mats with hidden holes supplied with kibble or treats foster natural foraging tendencies. Supervise use.

- **Obedience training** - Indoor training sessions develop physical and mental skills through practice cues, impulse control, and new tricks. Keep training positive and diverse.

- **Food puzzles** - Toys like Kongs loaded with parts of meals or treats transform eating into a task and engage Schnauzers for hours.

- **Nose work** - Hide scented items indoors and have your dog smell them out. This leverages their keen scenting skills for terrific mental tiring.

Exploring a selection of interactive toys and games with your Standard Schnauzer each day eliminates boredom and channels their energy into appropriate outlets for a satisfied, well-behaved companion.

Taking Your Schnauzer Hiking, Swimming etc.

Standard Schnauzers excel at different outdoor sporting activities thanks to their athleticism, stamina, and adaptable talents. Great possibilities include:

Hiking - With adequate conditioning, Schnauzers thrive on hiking's cerebral stimulation and exercise. Work increases distance gradually. Bring foldable bowls and plenty of water.

Swimming - Most Schnauzers love water play. Introduce swimming carefully ensuring your dog is comfortable. Always supervise and utilize a canine life jacket when boating.

Agility - With their lively, trainable disposition, Schnauzers tend to succeed at traversing agility courses. Classes provide wonderful bonding time through learning new talents together.

Flyball - This fast-paced relay-style racing game plays into the Schnauzer's prey drive and sprinting skills. Teams must hurdle leaps to trigger a ball launcher.

Nosework - Given their remarkable sense of smell, nosework games leverage your Schnauzer's keen scenting talents for an added cerebral workout.

Barn Hunt - Created for little terriers, barn hunt trials entail using nose work skills to discover hidden tubes holding rats, evaluating flexibility, drive, and searching ability.

Obedience/Rally Trials - Showcasing their proficient trainable nature, obedience, and rally trials challenge a Schnauzer's execution of timed handling maneuvers and obedience cues.

Tracking - The concentrated scenting abilities of Schnauzers permit success at tracking events requiring dogs to follow complex human scent trails over fields.

Schnauzers' diverse capabilities and people-pleasing nature allow them to flourish when trained in practically any canine sport or activity. Bond with your dog through their favorite physical and mental challenges.

Chapter Nine

Nutrition Tips for Schnauzers

Choosing a High-Quality Dog Food

Choosing nutritious food is vital for your Schnauzer's health. Look for these indications of a high-quality dog food:

- **Meat-based** - The first two ingredients should be quality animal protein sources like chicken, beef, fish, or eggs to boost muscle growth and energy.

- **Avoid fillers** - Avoid foods with maize, wheat, soy, by-products, or artificial colors/preservatives. These have minimal nutritional value.

- **Whole ingredients** - Foods with whole food elements like brown rice, barley, and sweet potatoes give more nutrients than fractionated grains and carbs.

- **Balanced formulation** - Ensure the meal is complete and balanced for all life stages according to AAFCO feeding experiments. This confirms nutritional sufficiency.

- **Appropriate calories** - Opt for dog food with an appropriate calorie density for your Schnauzer's lifestyle and age to maintain ideal weight.

- **Fatty acids** - Ingredient sources of omega fatty acids like fish, flaxseed and canola oil enhance skin/coat health and minimize inflammation.

- **Probiotics** - Live probiotics assist healthy digestion. Refrigerated and frozen foods may offer more effective probiotics.

- **Variety** - Rotating through 2-3 good quality foods delivers a diversity of nutrients while minimizing boredom.

- **Reputable brand** - Stick with brands that invest in research and meet stringent quality standards for safety and nutrition.

Consult your veterinarian if you have questions regarding the best food for your Schnauzer's unique needs. Feeding a premium diet is crucial for wellness.

Recommended Feeding Amounts

Standard Schnauzers should be fed a measured amount based on their size, age, and activity level. Some general feeding guidelines include:

- **Puppy** - Feed puppies 3-4 little meals daily. Provide at least 22 calories per pound of predicted adult body weight. Wean to 2 meals a day.

- **Adult** - Feed adult maintenance diet divided into 2 meals. Provide 30 calories per pound of goal body weight. Adjust up or down to maintain perfect condition.

- **Senior** - Reduce calories slightly for seniors about 7 years and older. Multiply weight by 28-30 calories per pound. Monitor weight attentively.

- **High activity** - Active Schnauzers need more fuel. Add 10-20% more calories with extra food or desserts.

- **Weight loss** - For overweight dogs, physicians recommend eating 60-75% of previous quantities to facilitate safe loss. Reassess often.

- **Pregnant/nursing** - Feed pregnant or nursing dams puppy chow and raise to 1.5 times regular amounts. Provide numerous smaller meals.

Always weigh out portions rather than estimate volume. This allows exact changes to maintain or achieve optimal body condition. Consult your vet if it is unclear how much to feed.

Supplements and Treats

While a decent core food should fulfill a Schnauzer's fundamental nutritional needs, several supplements might offer additional support:

- **Joint supplement** - Chondroprotective substances like glucosamine, chondroitin, and omega-3s enhance joint health and mobility. Helpful for older dogs.

- **Probiotic** - Live probiotic strains promote good digestion and immunity. Choose chilled items for optimal vitality.

- **Dental chews** - Chews containing anti-plaque substances clean teeth and freshen breath with regular usage. Help avoid periodontal disease.

- **Training treats** - Carry little soft snacks for walks and training sessions. Choose low-fat, low-sugar options such as boiled chicken, cheese, or commercial delights, limiting to 10% of daily calories.

- **Fruits/veggies** - Occasional nutrient-dense add-ins like blueberries, pumpkin, carrots, and broccoli provide antioxidants, fiber, and vitamins. Check safety for dogs first.

- **Avoid table food** - Leftover fatty meats, spices, onions, and other human foods might upset a

Schnauzer's stomach. Stick to dog-safe foods for treats.

When selecting vitamins or treats, always visit your veterinarian first to confirm they are safe and appropriate for your unique dog. An excellent diet is the cornerstone of good health.

Chapter Ten

Health and Veterinary Care

Signs of Illness to Watch For

Monitoring your Schnauzer for any irregularities or changes that may signal disease is vital for early action. Signs to check for include:

- **Loss of appetite** - An abrupt disinterest in food could signify an underlying health condition.

- **Weight fluctuations** - Sudden weight loss or gain needs inquiry from your veterinarian.

- **Lethargy** - Extreme tiredness, lack of interest in usual activities, or problems rising could suggest disease.

- **Coughing** - Persistent coughing or gagging may be an indication of respiratory distress and requires quick veterinary intervention.

- **Diarrhea/vomiting** - Repeated episodes of diarrhea or vomiting need medical attention for probable intestinal disorders. Withhold food initially.

- **Difficulty peeing** - Straining or weeping when trying to urinate is an emergency that could suggest obstruction requiring immediate veterinarian attention.

- **Skin changes** - Redness, hair loss, odor, or irritation can be indicators of dermatitis, infection, or parasites. Seek assessment.

- **Discharge** - Drainage from eyes, nose, or other regions generally suggests infection.

- **Limping** - Sudden limping after an injury or without apparent cause necessitates veterinary investigation to assess significance.

- **Seizures** - A seizure is a medical emergency requiring urgent veterinary attention. Time the episode and get aid promptly.

Be proactive about frequent vet exams to identify and address any health issues early. Learn your individual dog's typical baseline and look for variations that may signify a disease needing attention.

Vaccines and Preventative Care

Preventative veterinarian treatment is vital for safeguarding your Schnauzer's health. Recommendations include:

- **Core vaccines** - Rabies, distemper, parvovirus, and adenovirus vaccines are considered core for all dogs. Follow your veterinarian's protocol for boosters.

- **Non-core vaccines** - Leptospirosis, Lyme, bordetella, and canine influenza vaccines may be suggested based on lifestyle and location concerns. Discuss with your vet.

- **Parasite control** - Use monthly preventatives year-round to guard against fleas, ticks, heartworms, and intestinal parasites according to your vet's advice. Have annual fecal testing.

- **Dental care** - Daily teeth brushing, annual cleanings and dental x-rays can prevent periodontal disease.

- **Heartworm test** - Have an annual heartworm screening test to confirm your preventative medication is working properly.

- **Wellness screening** - Complete an annual wellness checkup involving a physical exam, blood work panel, urinalysis, and appraisal of body condition.

- **Genetic screening** - Consider having your Schnauzer screened for genetic problems common in the breed such as hip dysplasia, von Willebrand disease, and eye abnormalities.

Staying current on all recommended preventative veterinarian treatments preserves your Schnauzer's health and enjoyment of life at every stage. Discuss an appropriate plan with your trustworthy vet.

First Aid Basics

Having some basic first aid knowledge will help you respond effectively to frequent Schnauzer injuries until veterinary assistance is accessed:

Cuts and abrasions - Clean the wound gently with a saline rinse. Apply pressure with a clean cloth to control bleeding. Bandage and watch for signs of infection.

Burns - Flush chemical burns immediately with cool water. For thermal burns, try aloe vera gel or a cold compress. Seek veterinary attention for significant burns.

Bee stings – Remove the stinger if present. Apply a mixture of baking soda and water to calm the region. Give Benadryl if significant swelling. Watch for signs of anaphylaxis.

Choking - If your Schnauzer is fighting to breathe or choking uncontrollably, do canine Heimlich maneuver by gripping their abdomen and providing

5 forceful upward chest thrusts. Call the emergency vet ASAP.

Lameness - Restrict activities and reduce stairs/jumping to prevent worsening. Manage pain per your veterinarian's suggestions until the cause may be discovered.

Heat stroke - Move your overheated Schnauzer to shade, douse fur with cool (not cold) water, offer sips of water, and take it to the nearest veterinarian promptly. This is an emergency.

Seizure - Clear the area to avoid injury. Do not confine the dog or place anything in the mouth during a seizure. Time the occurrence until it passes then get veterinarian attention.

Knowing how to respond calmly in common crises can tremendously assist your Schnauzer until specialist veterinarian care is available. Build first aid knowledge and have a pet first aid kit on hand.

Chapter Eleven

The Joys of Living with a Schnauzer

The Loyal, Playful Schnauzer Temperament

The unusual disposition of the Schnauzer makes them a particularly entertaining companion. Their personality traits include:

Loyalty – Schnauzers create deep committed ties with their families. They seek to continually be by their owner's side. Their loving disposition makes them attentive friends.

Playfulness – Schnauzers keep a vibrant, mischievous side throughout life. They enjoy playing with family members, romping around, and delighting with their energetic actions.

Eager to Please - This trainable breed seeks to meet its owner's requests. They respond well to positive reinforcement training and are strongly motivated by praise, food rewards, and entertaining activities.

Alertness - Schnauzers have a cautious attitude and will rapidly announce visits at home or suspicious sights on walks with energetic barking. Their protective instincts are strong.

Courage - Despite their moderate stature, Schnauzers are exceptionally bold and fearless when challenged. They will place themselves between their family and any imagined threat.

Intelligence - The attentive, functioning intellect of the Schnauzer requires regular mental stimulation. They pick up on cues and routines rapidly. Without enough action they become bored.

Exuberance – Schnauzers attack life with passion and energy. They love to run, leap, play with abandon, and join in any family fun. Their bright energy is contagious.

The loyal, smart, fun-loving disposition of the Schnauzer makes them a great dog to live with when properly exercised and educated. Their soul and heart are bigger than their size.

Traveling with Your Dog

Standard Schnauzers are wonderful travel companions because of their compact size and ease of adapting to new situations. Tips for smooth trips:

- **Car trip** - Use a secured cage or restraint in the car. Stop every 2-3 hours to stretch your legs and relieve yourself. Never leave them unsupervised in automobiles.

- **Plane travel** - Get an airline-approved carrier and check requirements for carry-on vs cargo. Book direct flights during temperate months if possible.

- **Lodging** - Call ahead to check if chosen hotels welcome pets. Have moveable fencing to keep your Schnauzer isolated in rooms. Research neighboring outdoor relief locations.

- **Documentation** - Ensure your Schnauzer's identity tags are safe and their microchip is registered. Bring written documents of rabies vaccine and veterinary details.

- **Medication** - Talk to your veterinarian about whether relaxing medication or supplements may be useful to ease travel anxiety if needed.

- **Routine** - Try to stick to your Schnauzer's typical routine for feeding, walks, sleep cycles, and play as much as possible. Bring familiar toys and bedding.

- **First aid kit** - Pack a pet first aid kit with bandages, gauze, styptic powder, tweezers, antihistamine, saline, medical info, etc.

- **Safety** - Don't allow contact with unknown dogs. Keep your Schnauzer leashed anytime outside, including toilet walks at rest stops.

With proper planning, supplies, and proactive care, your Schnauzer may be a joyful traveling companion for trips close and far.

Enjoying Your Schnauzer's Golden Years

In their later senior years, Schnauzers require some adaptations to keep their lives pleasant and happy. Tips include:

- **More vet appointments** - See your veterinarian every 6 months for senior wellness checkups. Run annual blood panels, urinalysis, and other tests to stay ahead of age-related changes.

- **Weight management** - Monitor weight closely, as senior dogs are prone to gain. Adjust meals as needed to avoid obesity. Supplements may assist in maintaining muscle tone.

- **Joint support** - Chondroprotectants, physiotherapy, massages, and ramps/stairs can support mobility as arthritis develops. Keep up low-impact exercise.

- **Cognitive engagement** - Keep training and playing activities to stimulate their intellect. Try new toys and puzzles. Watch for any cognitive problems.

- **Diet improvements** - Switch to a high-quality senior diet. Add omega fatty acids and glucosamine supplements. Antioxidant foods support immunological function.

- **Dental care** - Senior dental cleanings and gum disease prevention are crucial for comfort. Brush regularly.

- **brushing** adjustments - If your Schnauzer struggles to stand for brushing, consider an elevated surface or sit/lie brushes. Keep their coats neat.

- **Nighttime care** - Consider reusable underpads if your senior is experiencing accidents at night. Allow access to sleep with you if they desire.

With thoughtful care adapted to the changing needs of your senior Schnauzer, their golden years can be filled with the continuous pleasure of family time, play, and long-lasting friendship.

20 homemade food recipe ideas for standard Schnauzer with ingredients and preparation instructions

1. Chicken and Rice Stew

Ingredients:

- 2 boneless, skinless chicken breasts (approximately 1 pound)
- 1 cup brown rice
- 1 sweet potato, diced
- 1 carrot, sliced
- 4 cups low-sodium chicken broth
- 1 tbsp olive oil

Instructions:

1. In a large pot, heat olive oil over medium heat.

2. Add chicken breasts and heat until browned on both sides, about 5 minutes per side.

3. Remove chicken from the pot and put aside.

4. In the same pot, add brown rice, sweet potato, carrot, and chicken broth.

5. Bring to a boil, then decrease heat to medium and simmer for 20 minutes, or until rice is cooked and vegetables are soft.

6. Shred the cooked chicken and return it back to the pot.

7. Allow the stew to cool before serving it to your Schnauzer.

2. Beef and Vegetable Stir-Fry

Ingredients:
- 1 pound lean ground beef
- 1 cup broccoli florets
- 1 bell pepper, diced
- 1 zucchini, sliced
- 2 tablespoons coconut oil

- 1 tablespoon low-sodium soy sauce

Instructions:

1. In a large skillet, heat coconut oil over medium heat.

2. Add ground beef and sauté until browned, breaking it apart with a spoon as it cooks.

3. Add broccoli, bell pepper, and zucchini to the skillet.

4. Cook for an additional 5-7 minutes, or until vegetables are soft.

5. Stir in soy sauce and simmer for another minute.

6. Allow the stir-fry to cool before serving it to your Schnauzer.

3. Salmon and Quinoa Delight

Ingredients:

- 2 salmon filets (approximately 1/2 pound)
- 1 cup quinoa
- 1 cup green beans, chopped
- 1/2 cup peas

- 2 tablespoons coconut oil

Instructions:

1. Preheat the oven to 400°F (200°C).

2. Place salmon filets on a baking pan lined with parchment paper.

3. Bake for 12-15 minutes, or until salmon is cooked through and flakes readily with a fork.

4. While the salmon is baking, cook quinoa according to package instructions.

5. In a separate saucepan, cook green beans and peas until soft.

6. In a large bowl, combine cooked quinoa, steaming vegetables, and coconut oil.

7. Flake the cooked salmon and gently stir it into the quinoa and veggie combination.

8. Allow the mixture to cool before serving it to your Schnauzer.

4. Turkey and Pumpkin Casserole

Ingredients:

- 1 pound minced turkey

- 1 cup pumpkin puree

- 1/2 cup rolled oats

- 1/4 cup grated cheese

- 1 egg

 - 1 tablespoon olive oil

Instructions:

1. Preheat the oven to 375°F (190°C).

2. In a large bowl, combine ground turkey, pumpkin puree, rolled oats, shredded cheese, and egg.

3. Mix until completely blended.

4. Grease a baking dish with olive oil and put the turkey mixture equally in the dish.

5. Bake for 25-30 minutes, or until the top is golden brown and the dish is cooked through.

6. Allow the casserole to cool before serving it to your Schnauzer.

5. Lamb and Potato Stew

Ingredients:

- 1 pound lamb stew meat

- 2 potatoes, diced

- 1 cup green peas

- 1/2 cup chopped parsley

- 4 cups low-sodium beef broth

- 1 tablespoon coconut oil

Instructions:

1. In a big pot, heat coconut oil over medium heat.

2. Add lamb stew meat and heat until browned on all sides.

3. Add diced potatoes, green peas, chopped parsley, and beef stock to the pot.

4. Bring to a boil, then decrease heat to low and simmer for 45-60 minutes, or until lamb is tender and potatoes are cooked through.

5. Allow the stew to cool before serving it to your Schnauzer.

6. Turkey and Vegetable Medley

Ingredients:

- 1 pound ground turkey

- 1 cup mixed veggies (carrots, peas, green beans), diced

 - 1/2 cup cooked brown rice

- 2 tablespoons olive oil

 - 1 teaspoon dried parsley

Instructions:

1. In a pan, heat olive oil over medium heat.

2. Add ground turkey and heat until browned, breaking it apart with a spoon.

3. Add mixed vegetables and simmer until soft, about 5-7 minutes.

4. Stir in cooked brown rice and dried parsley.

5. Cook for an additional 2-3 minutes.

6. Allow the mélange to cool before serving it to your Schnauzer.

7. Fish and Sweet Potato Cakes

Ingredients:

- 2 cans of tinned salmon or tuna

- 2 large sweet potatoes, boiled and mashed

- 1/2 cup oat flour

- 1 egg

- 1 tablespoon coconut oil

Instructions:

1. In a large bowl, combine canned salmon or tuna, mashed sweet potatoes, oat flour, and egg.

2. Mix until completely incorporated.

3. Form the ingredients into tiny patties.

4. In a skillet, heat coconut oil over medium heat.

5. Cook the patties for 3-4 minutes on each side, or until golden brown and cooked through.

6. Allow the cakes to cool before serving to your Schnauzer.

8. Beef and Barley Stew

Ingredients:

- 1 pound beef stew meat, cubed
- 1 cup barley
- 2 carrots, diced
- 1 celery stalk, chopped
- 4 cups low-sodium beef broth
- 1 tablespoon olive oil

Instructions:

1. In a big pot, heat olive oil over medium heat.

2. Add beef stew meat and sauté until browned on all sides.

3. Add barley, carrots, celery, and beef stock to the pot.

4. Bring to a boil, then decrease the heat to low and simmer for 1-1.5 hours, or until beef is tender and barley is cooked.

5. Allow the stew to cool before serving it to your Schnauzer.

9. Chicken and Veggie Meatballs

Ingredients:

- 1 pound minced chicken

- 1 cup shredded zucchini

- 1/2 cup grated carrot

- 1/4 cup finely chopped spinach

- 1/4 cup grated Parmesan cheese

- 1 egg

Instructions:

1. Preheat the oven to 375°F (190°C).

2. In a large bowl, add ground chicken, grated zucchini, grated carrot, chopped spinach, Parmesan cheese, and egg.

3. Mix until completely blended.

4. Roll the mixture into tiny meatballs and set them on a baking sheet lined with parchment paper.

5. Bake for 20-25 minutes, or until cooked through.

6. Allow the meatballs to cool before serving to your Schnauzer.

10. Pork and Apple Casserole

Ingredients:

- 1 pound lean pork loin, cubed
- 2 apples, peeled and diced
- 1 cup cooked quinoa
- 1/2 cup frozen peas
- 1/4 cup chopped parsley
- 1 tablespoon coconut oil

Instructions:

1. Preheat the oven to 375°F (190°C).

2. In a skillet, heat coconut oil over medium heat.

3. Add pork loin pieces and heat until browned on all sides.

4. In a large bowl, add cooked pork loin, diced apples, cooked quinoa, frozen peas, and chopped parsley.

5. Transfer the mixture to a prepared baking dish.

6. Bake for 25-30 minutes, or until cooked through.

7. Allow the casserole to cool before serving it to your Schnauzer.

11. Lamb and Rice Pilaf

Ingredients:

- 1 pound ground lamb

- 1 cup cooked white rice

- 1/2 cup chopped carrots

- 1/2 cup green peas

- 2 tablespoons olive oil

- 1 teaspoon dried oregano

Instructions:

1. In a pan, heat olive oil over medium heat.

2. Add ground lamb and heat until browned, breaking it apart with a spoon.

3. Add diced carrots and simmer for 3-4 minutes until slightly cooked.

4. Stir in green peas and cooked white rice.

5. Season with dry oregano and simmer for a further 2-3 minutes.

6. Allow the pilaf to cool before serving it to your Schnauzer.

12. Turkey and Lentil Stew

Ingredients:

- 1 pound mince turkey

- 1 cup dried lentils, rinsed

- 2 carrots, diced

- 1 celery stalk, chopped

- 4 cups low-sodium vegetable broth

- 1 tablespoon coconut oil

Instructions:

1. In a big pot, heat coconut oil over medium heat.

2. Add ground turkey and heat until browned.

3. Add dried lentils, diced carrots, chopped celery, and vegetable broth to the pot.

4. Bring to a boil, then decrease heat to low and simmer for 30-40 minutes, or until lentils are cooked.

5. Allow the stew to cool before serving it to your Schnauzer.

13. Chicken and Pumpkin Soup

Ingredients:

- 2 boneless, skinless chicken breasts

- 1 cup pumpkin puree

- 1/2 cup chopped potatoes

- 1/2 cup chopped green beans

- 4 cups low-sodium chicken broth

- 1 tablespoon olive oil

Instructions:

1. In a large pot, heat olive oil over medium heat.

2. Add chicken breasts and heat until browned on both sides.

3. Remove chicken from the pot and put aside.

4. Add pumpkin puree, diced potatoes, chopped green beans, and chicken stock to the pot.

5. Bring to a boil, then decrease heat to medium and simmer for 20-25 minutes, or until vegetables are cooked.

6. Shred the cooked chicken and return it back to the pot.

7. Allow the soup to cool before serving to your Schnauzer.

14. Beef and Pumpkin Stew

Ingredients:

- 1 pound beef stew meat, cubed

- 1 cup pumpkin chunks

- 1/2 cup chopped kale

- 1/2 cup cooked quinoa

- 4 cups low-sodium beef broth

- 1 tablespoon coconut oil

Instructions:

1. In a big pot, heat coconut oil over medium heat.

2. Add beef stew meat and sauté until browned on all sides.

3. Add pumpkin chunks, chopped kale, cooked quinoa, and beef broth to the pot.

4. Bring to a boil, then decrease heat to low and simmer for 1-1.5 hours, or until beef is cooked.

5. Allow the stew to cool before serving it to your Schnauzer.

15. Turkey and Cranberry Meatballs

Ingredients:

- 1 pound minced turkey

- 1/2 cup dried cranberries, roughly chopped

- 1/4 cup almond flour

 - 1 egg

- 1 tablespoon olive oil

Instructions:

1. Preheat the oven to 375°F (190°C).

2. In a large bowl, combine ground turkey, chopped dried cranberries, almond flour, and egg.

3. Mix until completely blended.

4. Roll the mixture into tiny meatballs and set them on a baking sheet lined with parchment paper.

5. Brush the meatballs with olive oil.

6. Bake for 20-25 minutes, or until cooked through.

7. Allow the meatballs to cool before serving to your Schnauzer.

16. Salmon and Sweet Potato Chowder

Ingredients:

- 2 salmon filets (approximately 1/2 pound)

 - 2 sweet potatoes, diced

- 1 cup chopped broccoli

- 4 cups low-sodium vegetable broth

- 1 tablespoon coconut oil

Instructions:

1. In a big pot, heat coconut oil over medium heat.

2. Add diced sweet potatoes and chopped broccoli to the pot and sauté for 5 minutes.

3. Pour in veggie broth and bring to a boil.

4. Reduce heat to medium and simmer for 15 minutes, or until vegetables are soft.

5. Meanwhile, bake or simmer the fish until cooked through.

6. Flake the cooked fish and add it to the saucepan.

7. Simmer for an additional 5 minutes.

8. Allow the chowder to cool before serving it to your Schnauzer.

17. Chicken and Blueberry Salad

Ingredients:

- 2 boneless, skinless chicken breasts

- 1 cup blueberries

- 1 cup chopped spinach

- 1/4 cup plain Greek yogurt

- 1 tablespoon honey

Instructions:

1. Cook the chicken breasts until thoroughly done and dice them into bite-sized pieces.

2. In a large bowl, add diced chicken, blueberries, chopped spinach, Greek yogurt, and honey.

3. Mix until completely blended.

4. Serve the salad cold in your Schnauzer.

18. Beef and Carrot Casserole

Ingredients:

- 1 pound lean ground beef

- 2 cups chopped carrots

- 1 cup cooked quinoa

- 1/2 cup grated cheese

- 1 egg

- 1 tablespoon olive oil

Instructions:

1. Preheat the oven to 375°F (190°C).

2. In a pan, heat olive oil over medium heat.

3. Add ground meat and heat until browned.

4. In a large bowl, combine cooked ground beef, diced carrots, cooked quinoa, grated cheese, and egg.

5. Mix until completely blended.

6. Transfer the mixture to a prepared baking dish.

7. Bake for 25-30 minutes, or until heated through and golden brown on top.

8. Allow the casserole to cool before serving it to your Schnauzer.

19. Turkey and Cranberry Stuffed Peppers

Ingredients:

- 1 pound minced turkey

- 4 bell peppers

- 1/2 cup dried cranberries, finely chopped

 - 1/2 cup cooked brown rice

- 1/4 cup minced parsley

- 1 tablespoon coconut oil

Instructions:

1. Preheat the oven to 375°F (190°C).

2. Cut the tops off the bell peppers and remove the seeds and membranes.

3. In a skillet, heat coconut oil over medium heat.

4. Add ground turkey and heat until browned.

5. In a large bowl, combine cooked ground turkey, chopped dried cranberries, cooked brown rice, and chopped parsley.

6. Stuff the mixture into the bell peppers.

7. Place the filled peppers in a baking tray and cover with foil.

8. Bake for 25-30 minutes, or until peppers are tender.

9. Allow the stuffed peppers to cool before serving to your Schnauzer.

20. Lamb and Green Bean Stir-Fry

Ingredients:

- 1 pound lamb leg steak, thinly sliced - 2 cups green beans, trimmed and halved

- 1 bell pepper, sliced

- 2 teaspoons soy sauce

- 1 tablespoon sesame oil

- 1 teaspoon minced garlic

Instructions:

1. In a large skillet or wok, heat sesame oil over medium-high heat.

2. Add minced garlic and stir-fry for 1 minute.

3. Add sliced lamb and heat until browned.

4. Add green beans and bell pepper slices to the skillet.

5. Stir in soy sauce and continue to stir-fry until veggies are soft and meat is cooked through.

6. Allow the stir-fry to cool before serving it to your Schnauzer.

Note